How to use this book 

Follow the advice, in italics, given for you on each page.
Support the children as they read the text that is shaded in cream.
Praise *the children at every step!*
Detailed guidance is provided in the Read Write Inc. Phonics Handbook.

9 reading activities

Children:

1 *Practise reading the speed sounds.*
2 *Read the green, red and challenge words for the non-fiction text.*
3 *Listen as you read the introduction.*
4 *Discuss the vocabulary check with you.*
5 *Read the non-fiction text.*
6 *Re-read the non-fiction text and discuss the 'questions to talk about'.*
7 *Re-read the non-fiction text with fluency and expression.*
8 *Answer the questions to 'read and answer'.*
9 *Practise reading the speed words.*

Speed sounds

Consonants *Say the pure sounds (do not add 'uh').*

f ff	l (ll) le	m mm	n nn kn	r rr wr	s ss c ce	v ve	z zz (se) s	sh	th	ng nk

b bb	c k (ck)	d dd	g gg gu	h	j	p (pp)	qu	t tt	w (wh)	x	y	ch tch

Vowels *Say the vowel sound and then the word, eg 'a', 'at'.*

at	hen head	in	on	up	day make	see tea happy he	high smile lie find	blow home no

zoo	look	car	for door snore	fair	whirl	shout	boy spoil

*Each box contains one sound but sometimes more than one grapheme. Focus graphemes are **circled**.*

Green words

Read in Fred Talk (pure sounds).

safe	while	ride	bike	size	time	quite	price
side	ice	slide	white	right	night	might	check
read	must	switch	back	street	snow	slip	ch oo se
when	bell						

Read in syllables.

foll`ow → follow    guide`lines → guidelines   be`fore → before

trou`sers → trousers    hel`met → helmet   traff`ic → traffic

for`get → forget    pave`ment → pavement

Read the root word first and then with the ending.

brake → brakes   light → lights   skirt → skirts

wh eel → wh eels   trap → trapped

Red words

Challenge words

On your bike

Introduction

Do you have a bike? Do you know how to ride safely? This book will tell you all you need to know about having fun and being safe on your bike.

Written by Gill Munton

Vocabulary check

Discuss the meaning (as used in the non-fiction text) after the children have read the word.

<table>
<tr><td></td><td>**definition**</td></tr>
<tr><td>**guidelines**</td><td>*rules or suggestions on how to do something*</td></tr>
<tr><td>**to dress**</td><td>*to put on clothes*</td></tr>
<tr><td>**price**</td><td>*how much something costs*</td></tr>
</table>

Punctuation to note:

You Before	
	Capital letters that start sentences
.	*Full stop at the end of each sentence*
:	*Colon to show a list will follow*
–	*Dash to show that there is more to read about what has already been said*
!	*Exclamation marks to show that something is very important*

In this book, you can read about how to be safe while you ride your bike.
Follow the guidelines!

Your bike

Before you ride your bike, check:

Your bike must be the right size – not too big and not too small.

When you ride your bike at night time, you must switch on your lights.

You need a white light at the front and a red light at the back.

How to dress

Put on shorts or tight trousers.

No long skirts or wide trousers – they might get trapped in the wheels.

You can get a helmet for quite a low price.

Check that your helmet fits well.

Put on your helmet each time you ride your bike.

13

How to ride your bike

Ride at the side of the street, next to the pavement.

Do not ride your bike on a street with lots of traffic.

Do not ride your bike in ice and snow.
Your wheels might slip and slide.

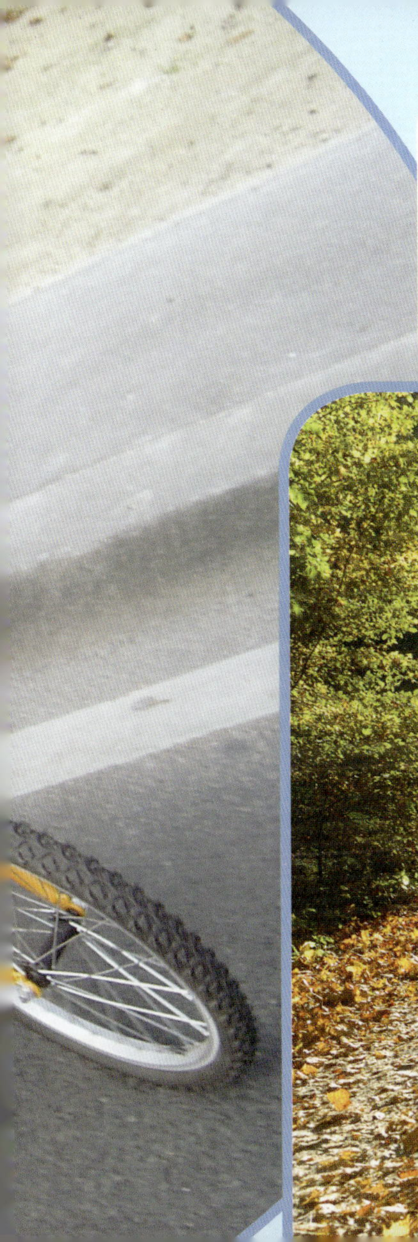

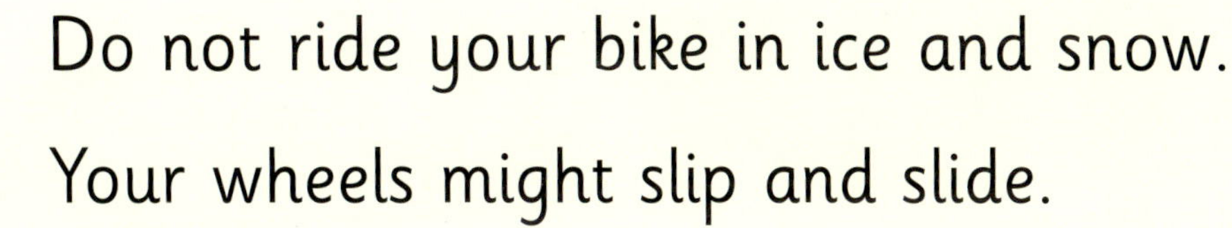

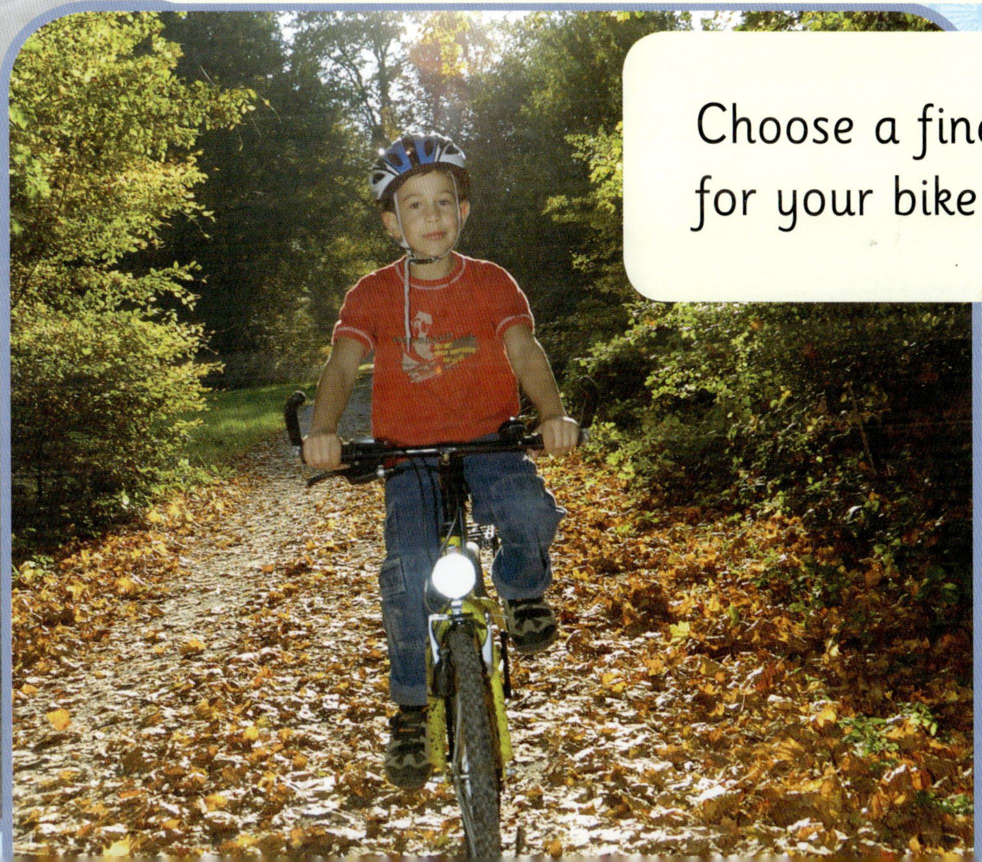

Choose a fine day
for your bike ride.

Don't forget – be
safe when you
ride your bike!

Questions to talk about 

Re-read the page. Read the question to the children. Tell them whether it is a FIND IT *question or* PROVE IT *question.*

<table>
<tr><td>

FIND IT
✓ *Turn to the page*
✓ *Read the question*
✓ *Find the answer*

</td><td>

PROVE IT
✓ *Turn to the page*
✓ *Read the question*
✓ *Find your evidence*
✓ *Explain why*

</td></tr>
</table>

Page 9:	PROVE IT	*What is this book about?*
Page 10:	FIND IT	*What is important about the size of your bike?*
Page 11:	FIND IT	*What sort of lights do you need on your bike?*
Page 12:	PROVE IT	*Do you think it's safe to wear baggy trousers on a bike?*
Page 13:	FIND IT	*What is it important to check when choosing a helmet?*
Page 14:	FIND IT	*Where on the street should you ride your bike?*
Page 15:	PROVE IT	*Do you think it's safe to ride in the snow?*

Questions to read and answer 

(Children complete without your help.)

1 What do the guidelines in this book tell you?

2 What do you check on your bike before you ride it?

3 What might happen if you have a long skirt or wide trousers on when you ride your bike?

4 What sort of day is safe for a bike ride?

5 What must you put on your head each time you ride your bike?